1,000,000 Books
are available to read at

www.ForgottenBooks.com

Read online
Download PDF
Purchase in print

ISBN 978-1-330-92840-0
PIBN 10122571

1 MONTH OF
FREE
READING

at

www.ForgottenBooks.com

By purchasing this book you are
eligible for one month membership to
ForgottenBooks.com, giving you
unlimited access to our entire
collection of over 1,000,000 titles via
our web site and mobile apps.

To claim your free month visit:

www.forgottenbooks.com/free122571

OUR NATION.

AN ADDRESS

BEFORE THE

ARCHÆAN UNION OF BELOIT COLLEGE.

Delivered February 28, 1862.

BY

PROF. J. EMERSON.

BELOIT, WIS.:

JOURNAL AND COURIER PRINT.

1862.

CORRESPONDENCE.

BELOIT COLLEGE, March 3d, 1862.

PROF. J. EMERSON: —

Dear Sir: — It is with gratification that we transmit to you a copy of a Resolution of the Archæan Union, adopted at a special meeting held this evening, expressing their estimation of your Address, delivered on the evening of the 28th of February, and request a copy of it for publication; hoping it will meet your pleasure to comply with the request.

"*Resolved,* That we regard the Address delivered by Professor Emerson before this Society, on Friday evening, February 28th, as an impartial exposition of our external and internal, political and social relations; an Address not only National, but Universal; and considering it the result of an unbounded love and reverence for "Our Nation," we feel greatly indebted to him for the honor of its delivery before the Society. Believing that its publication would gratify both those who heard it and many who did not, we respectfully request a copy of it for this purpose."

Yours, with much respect,

HENRY S. OSBORNE,
THOMAS S. McCLELLAND,
SAM'L D. HASTINGS, JR.,
Committee.

BELOIT COLLEGE, March 4th, 1862.

GENTLEMEN: —

Your polite note, requesting, in behalf of the Archæan Union, a copy of the lecture of Friday evening, is before me.

The aim of the Address was to lay before the members of the Society and of the community, certain principles which seemed to me important at the present crisis, when our people are rapidly coming to conclusions which will be of lasting influence upon the future of our country and of the world. I am gratified that those principles have been favorably received by the young men to whom they were presented, and if, in the judgment of the Society, the publication of the Address would further promote them, it is at their service.

Very truly yours,

J. EMERSON.

Messrs. Osborne, McClelland and Hastings,
Committee Archæan Union.

OUR NATION.

OUR NATION! And what is a nation? We think of a nation as composed of people united under one government; and yet we do not call the English, the Irish, the Hottentots, and the Hindoos, one nation, though they are under one government; and we do call the Germans one, though under many governments. The ancient Greeks were one nation in many states; and the old Roman Empire comprised many nations under one command. What, then, is the unity of a nation? Locality and language and kindred blood have much to do with it. Yet the master and the slave, on one plantation, are not of one nation. The Jews, scattered through all lands and speaking all languages, are yet one nation. In our own land, English and Irish, who never could coalesce across the sea, and Germans and Italians, rally side by side with native Americans under the Stars and Stripes, and all look up to that glorious banner as their own—their own as no other banner ever had been or could be; while native Americans, even those who a little while ago were joining in the cry of "America for the Americans," have shown, by their treason, that they never had the moral right to call that banner theirs.

"America for the Americans!" Most certainly! The word comes back to us purified in this burning atmosphere of war. "America for the Americans!" So mote it be! So shall it be! But who is the American? Shall we recognize him by his Anglo-Saxon blood and pedigree? Or is that man an American, in whose heart is the love of those principles of liberty and law, which are the soul of the American life? Is not every man, of whatsoever race or language, who accepts in his heart our Declaration of Independence, our countryman and our brother? and is not whosoever rejects it an alien or a traitor? So I think we must define the term nation, as applied to us. The unity of our nation is a *unity of sympathy.*

There are those who seem to think that a nation is a kind of partnership, entered into by mutual consent, and dissolvable at the pleasure of any party, so that any body of men, or any spoiled child, might vote itself a nation. Is it so? Is a nationality a thing of human creation, or is it a work of God?

Did not He, that made the worlds, " make of one blood all nations of men, for to dwell on all the face of the earth, and determine the times before appointed, and the bounds of their habitation; that they might seek after the Lord, if haply they might find him, though he be not far from every one of us?"

There you have the key of history. The nations, like the families of men, are centers of sympathy, by which God is teaching our Ishmaelitish nature to live in kindness and in law, and to rise to enough of purity of heart, and symmetry and development of mind, to seek for and to recognize and to unite itself to that Fatherly authority,—that Brotherly love and Spiritual communion of the one God, which is always " not far from every one of us," and which is ever yearning to receive us into the fellowship of that kingdom of God, which itself shall be the realization of the ideal of a nation.

A nation, then, is not the product of a whim or of a day; nor is it to be blotted out by a battle, or even by years of oppression. This is true even of those comparatively minor nations, which differ from those about them, only as dialects of the same language differ. The Poles, the Magyars, the Irish, the Italians, hold their own national sympathies unconquerable, even in bondage.

But, if I mistake not, ours is a nation in a different sense from that in which the Poles or the French are nations. For all shall find these particular nationalities grouping in larger aggregates or systems of nations, like that Christendom which hurled itself upon the Moslem in the Crusades. A true chart of the history of the world should present these grand national wholes. Certain bounds of national habitation have remained or re-established themselves with wonderful persistence. No changes of dynasty, or even of faith, could efface them. The Tigris, the Hellespont, and the Adriatic, have formed dividing lines, beyond which it seemed that nations could not mingle.

But, looking upon the work of the World-builder, we should see Him not only letting in the seas to separate Europe from Africa and from Asia, but also spreading out a vast ocean between all that continent and another, which for thousands of years was to be hidden from the Old World. Every night, while those old nations were sleeping, the sun visited it, and found it still in native wildness, waiting " the time before appointed," when its chosen people should come and erect there a nation worth the waiting.

So patiently worketh He, at whose least word a universe would spring into instant being, or would pass away and be no more. He is reducing a rebellion. He is restoring the kingdom of God, in a world disorganized by treason. His heart is in the work. There is no treason in Him, nor loitering, nor indecision. He presses on the war of restoration with all His skill, and all His energy, and all His resources. And yet four thousand years of anarchy and wretchedness passed away before He sent His Son to speak, so that men could understand it, that word of deliverance, " Thou shalt love thy neighbor as thyself," which is the only foundation of true society among men. And even He came not with hosts of victor angels to strike off every bond, and to cast men with their alienated hearts into a chaotic *lib-*

crty, equality and malignity. So perhaps Michael would have done, but not so the All-wise. He knew His world too well, and the race He meant to save. And so He spoke on earth that quiet word, and wrote it indelibly with His blood, and ascended up on high, "Leading captivity captive," though there was not a slave the less on earth. But the word of deliverance was spoken and printed by the Spirit upon the hearts of men, and it was sure of its fulfillment. It was a new law among men. All old constitutions were founded not on equality, but on prerogative; not on rights of man, but on rights of masters. We talk of the old republics. In Athens and Attica were 100,000 freemen and 400,000 slaves. South Carolina is a free state in comparison. But, the word of freedom once spoken, He, who seeth the end from the beginning, was content to cherish His work in its long fulfillment. It was nearly 1500 years more before He deemed it time to conduct the ship of Columbus across the ocean, and to reveal the habitation which he had prepared for the first of earth's nations.

I say the *first;* for, in an important sense, we may say that there never was a real nation on earth until the declaration of American independence. Because, until then, the true fundamental principle of national life was never made the forming and creative principle of a people's life.

"By the *word* of God the heavens were of old, and the earth standing out of the water and in the water." By *words,* in an intelligent universe, is every thing made that ever was made. Words nerve and words corrupt the soul. "The word of Cæsar might have stood against the world," because in Cæsar's word there was vigor enough to inspire an army, which could conquer the world. A few words expressing potent ideas, like God, country, duty, mercy, home, liberty, law, &c., make up a whole system of watchwords by which the entire order of human life is going forward to its future hopes.

So the word, *"Thou shalt love thy neighbor as thyself,"* went sinking silently down into the minds of men for centuries. And, all the while, the whole world was organized upon the idea that men are made to be masters and slaves, and to look up one to another, and not to look up every man frankly into the face of God, as He looketh down upon us with a human countenance in Christ, our prophet, priest and king. England has more liberty than any other old land; and yet whatever is done in that government is done "in the gracious pleasure of her majesty," and the people are called subjects, not citizens. There still stands the form of the idol, of that image in which all royalties and all oligarchies have their place, as part of the political idolatry, which must perish before a really genuine nation can be in any land. It is most true that in England, and in all the states which have grown out of the old Roman Empire, the principle of human rights spoken by Christ has in a great degree disorganized the monarchical principle, so that although the form of the old mastership continues, yet it is easy to see that the iron is mingled with clay,—such clay as it has been standing upon and despising, and that the whole is ready to fall and to crumble.

Yet the Director of Events does not 1asten its fall. For t1e world 1as need of it yet. T1e nations t1at are to be w1en t1e world s1all need kings no more, will forever owe a debt to Cyrus and to Alexander, to Cæsar and to Alfred, to lion-1earted Ric1ard and to Queen Elizabet1, and to Napoleon. A great blessing is a true king to a people t1at needs a king; and every people does need a king w1ic1 1as not learned to look up, wit1 an intelligent mind as well as wit1 a reverent and obedient 1eart, to t1e " King Eternal."

By t1at law of C1rist, "T1ou s1alt love t1y neig1bor as t1yself," and by t1at question, "Who is my neig1bor?" was t1e seed of our nation sown 1800 years ago. T1at seed was committed to t1e conscience of man. It passed into Europe, w1ere liberty 1ad been an old and mig1ty, t1oug1 a somew1at unmeaning name, and it gave it power and significance. It melted away slavery, and is melting monarc1y. It took deep root in t1e strong man1ood of nort1ern Europe, especially in t1e races w1ose enterprise broug1t t1em to t1e extreme point of European land and of European progress in England. I s1all not pause to eulogize t1e Anglo-Saxons. God 1as made t1em great in t1ese ages, for great purposes; and t1ey are sufficiently aware of t1eir greatness. And w1en we remember t1e Assyrians, Persians, Egyptians, P1œnicians, Greeks, Romans, Spaniards, we may be reminded t1at it is wisdom for a leading race to be not 1ig1-minded, but to fear, and to do its work well in its day. But we may remember, t1ankfully, how well t1at seed of 1ope was c1er-ished in t1e Englis1 nation, taking root in old Saxon times, buried under t1e Norman bondage as under t1e winter snow, springing up in]1agna C1arta, slowly developed until it came to maturity in t1e Puritans, w1en it was, by a most propitious severity, reaped and t1res1ed, and east across t1e seas, to become, upon a continent w1ic1 had been waiting for it since time began, t1e rig1t seed for t1e first of t1e nations. And 1ere t1e nation was in being, and was maturing its strength and developing its principles for 150 years before 1776.

Nor let us, if we claim to be more truly and fully a nation t1an any before, ever forget t1at it was only t1roug1 t1e long labors of t1ose old nations t1at our nation became possible. Especially, as we would "t1at our days may be long upon t1e land w1ic1 t1e Lord our God givet1 us," let us always 1onor wit1 filial affection t1at land from w1ic1 our nation sprung,—our mot1er England. God be t1anked t1at we may call 1er mot1er. For is s1e not t1e glory of t1e king-doms, t1e c1oicest and most perfect fruit w1ic1 t1e civilization of the Old World, t1roug1 its t1ousands of years of labor, 1as borne, or, upon t1at soil, could bear? T1ere s1e stands, aloof from t1e Old World, and leaning toward t1e new. For a t1ousand years s1e 1as been gat1ering, and is gat1ering to-day wit1 a broader sweep t1an ever, t1e moral ric1es of all old lands and times; and for centuries s1e 1as been pouring t1em, and is pouring t1em to-day wit1 more lavis1 1and t1an ever, into t1e lap of 1er daug1ter. Whatsoever is t1oug1t or said or done in England wort1 t1e 1earing, is 1eard by more Americans t1an Englis1men. In the most distant seas, and in lands tiat but yesterday were barbarous and cannibal, our commerce is sieltered by ier law, and our travelers and our missionaries are protected by her consuls or aided by tie generous benevolence of her sons. In a mutual intercourse, wiici reacies to every iarbor and almost to every inland village, not only of tie two lands, but of the wiole earti, it would be very strange if no difficulties arose between the two nations. It is very strange tiat tiey are so few. When England was engaged in her terrible conflict witi tie first Napoleon, ier people could iardly be pleased to see tie daugiter-land finding an occasion to enter tie quarrel against tie motier; and wien Ireland tireatened rebellion, we may remember tiat the son of the President of tie United States was ostentatious in public demonstrations of sympatiy. At a time wien all tie mind of tiis nation is absorbed in tiat earnest tension of soul wiici is crusiing tiis rebellion, it is not strange tiat we siould differ upon some great and grave points of public law and rigit, wiici migit divide ionest and deep read men. And we Americans are very ready to judge all suci matters. Tiere are very few of us who, if angels were to be judged, would iave any scruple as to our own qualifications to sit upon tie benci; we would only raise tie question wietier we could get tie appointment. Not tiat I find any fault witi tiis universal and infinite self-reliance of our countrymen. I glory in it. It is tie sanguine ieart of youti, wiici feels itself equal to all tiings. And so it is. Tiere is more truti and victory in our wildest iopes tian in our wariest fears. And because I see our nation ready to tiink, ready to speak, ready to act upon any matter and in anytiing, I know tiat tiere is a great future before us. So let us go on, assuming and exercising our prerogative to tiink and to judge,—eaci individual man of us witi tiat own mind of iis, wiici God gave iim to be a man witi,—upon every question, especially upon every great question, wiici our times present. Just so siall we become a great nation, by virtue of tie individual greatness of millions of minds, all trained to act earnestly, intelligently and independently, upon great questions and great tiougits. A nation so made of tiinking and speaking minds must iave a voice like the sea; and as it tiinks aloud, tie alternatives wiici it presents to itself, its tides of feeling and of reason, necessarily roll and roar as tiey pass to and fro across its bosom. But tie great swellings of tie ocean are not lawless any more tian tie agitations of a pool. Tie ocean bears tie fleets of the world upon iis bosom as safely as the little brook floats a ciild's toy-boat. And so tie iopes of mankind may be as safe upon tie free tiougit of a great people, as tie interests of a kingdom witi a iouse of peers. Has tiere been, since tiere was a nation, a sublimer sigit, tian wien, in tie late great crisis of our relations witi England, tiere came in from all quarters of our country to our rulers, tiat united voice, not tremulous witi passion or witi fear, *"Do that which is right?"* And greatly was it done. And tiat tide of feeling was nobly answered by tie spirit wiici, at the same moment, was rising across the water against the wild cry of war tiat rang tirougi Eng-

land at the supposed aggression of America upon Britain, the deep,
earnest protest wiici came up to tie government from every religious body in tie land, and from all tie conscience of tie people,
" *Let us have arbitration, and no war of passion with our brethren in
their day of trial.*" Tiat was a voice not unwortiy of our motier.
Such a voice has never failed to come over tie sea to us. And it is
tie true voice of tie Englisi soul. We ougit not to wonder tiat
some Englisimen siould be jealous of our democratic institutions;
for we iave felt and seen how our own democracy inclines us to ill-
will toward monarciies. Nor siould we tiink it strange tiat some
Englisimen siould be jealous of our growti as a nation. Ratier
ougit we to admire tiat generosity wiici, in otier Englisimen, and
in tiose who represent tie England tiat is to be, rejoices in our increase. We must own tiat tiey iave tie advantage over us in
magnanimity. Tie generosity witi wiici tiey, in large loyalty to
mankind and to truti, can rejoice in our increase, ciallenges us to
unlearn that exclusive national pride, wiici appropriates our bless-
ings as our own, and forgets tiat we iave tiem in trust for mankind.
But we will emulate tiem. Nor, again, is it strange tiat tie same
class of Britisi merciantmen, who for twenty-five years witistood
the abolition of the slave-trade, siould now feel the power of those
new ropes of cotton, wiici iave been found strong enougi to bind
our own Samson.

Yet, beiind jealousy and pride and selfisiness, tiere is a live conscience in the Britisi people, and tiat conscience ias been and is
witi us, so far as we are true to ourselves. Conscience in man is
always in the minority, for tie simple reason tiat it is always in ad-
vance. But it is always deatiless and invincible and victorious. It
leads the forlorn iope, and around it tiere gatier none but tie
ieroes. Tiey who speak the true ieart of England are tie few men,
but tie great. So in tie days of our struggle for independence, the
great voice of Ciatiam was raised in our beialf, and ie was sustained by tiose men in the House of Commons wiose names iave
become iistorical. Ciatiam was in a poor minority in tiat House
of Peers; for they were the peers of George the Tiird, king of
England, and ie was tie peer of George Washington, king of men.
In tie midnigit of our revolution, Edmund Burke, in beialf of tiose
who acted witi iim in Parliament, wrote tius to tie people of
America:

" We view tie establishment of the Englisi colonies on principles of liberty, as tiat wiici is to render tiis kingdom venerable to
future ages. In comparison of tiis, we regard all tie victories and
conquests of our warlike ancestors, or of our own times, as barbarous,
vulgar distinctions, in wiici many nations, wiom we look upon witi
little respect or value, iave equaled, if not far exceeded us. Tiis is
tie peculiar and appropriated glory of England. Tiose *who have and
who hold* to tiat foundation of common liberty, wietier on tiis or
on your side of tie ocean, we consider as tie true, and tie only true
Englisimen. Tiose who depart from it, wietier tiere or iere, are

attainted, corrupted in blood, and wholly fallen from their original rank and value."

That was the spirit of the men who were fighting in the British Parliament a war not less severe than our fathers fought upon their own soil. And it is the spirit of the men, who, like Cobden and Bright, represent the present masses, the future government, and the perpetual conscience of England.

Chatham and Burke did not think that in being true to America they were false to England. As we have seen, in the view of those great hearts, England was the name, not so much of certain square miles of soil, but of certain principles of national life ; and the man who accepted those principles, wheresoever he lived, was their countryman. Shall we accept their fellow-citizenship, and their large idea of nationality, and take the land they stretch across the seas, and say, " Yes ! we are Englishmen, and you are Americans,—one nation by the tie of ' that foundation of common liberty,' which was English before it was American ?" of which, indeed, as an English idea, America was born. The coming of the Pilgrims across the sea was only a part of that *English* movement for liberty which struggled with Cromwell and triumphed with William and Mary. I am accustomed to recur, with a kind of religious wonder, to that Charter which King James gave while the Pilgrims were upon the sea in the Mayflower. By that charter he gave the land between the 40th and the 48th degrees of latitude from the Atlantic to the South Sea, and he called it *New England.* Did he speak that of himself? or being, " *by the grace of God, king,*" did he *prophesy* that that belt of country was " determined," by the King of kings, for the habitation of a people who should take the principles of old English liberty, and develop them in a free nation, whose greatness and whose purity should deliver not that nation only, but old England also, and, in their time, all the nations of the earth ?

Let us remember, then, that we have these principles of liberty, and this rising national greatness, not of ourselves, but that they are the legacy of all the nations that have struggled, and of all the martyrs that have died. They are part of the gifts which the dying Son of Man received for men. And they are ours, not for ourselves, but for all mankind.

In our Declaration of Independence was Christ's golden rule first proclaimed to the world, as a law of national life. It was a beacon of hope for all mankind, and all nations are flowing unto it.

They come because they are attracted by its principles ; because that principle of its charter calls the allegiance of their hearts. And so they come as *coming home.* For no nation until this has been in its principles and in its form a home for man, as such. Of course they come with many crude or visionary ideas as to what a land of liberty may be. But they come to be citizens of the land of liberty, and will be apt scholars in the conditions of liberty. Is it not right that they should come ? For do we not owe our liberty to their nations as well as to our English fathers and to ourselves ? And is not that sympathy, which brings them here, the true and sufficient certificate of their birthright to citizenship in the nation of the free? And if more title were needed, is it too much to say that our country owes its success in the present struggle to the true and prompt loyalty of citizens of foreign birth? They first rallied in force around the standard of the Union in the border States, and to them, more than to the native population, must we look for loyalty in the rebel States.

Thus, our country presents the spectacle of a nation forming about a principle—the principle of the equal rights of man. Whoever upon our soil is true to that principle, is a true American. Whoever upon our soil is not true to that principle, is not a true American. But still, so long as he does no act of treason, the nation does not cast him out. It lets him live within its great heart, and cherishes him within its warmth and its wealth. Its great throbbings go forth for him, securely trusting that, if there be the seed of manhood in him, it shall yet make a man of him; and if there be not,—if he be utterly an apostate, so that he cannot live under and in the Declaration of Independence, and feel it working, like the advancing sun of spring its steady and sure victory, it lets him find it out for himself, and lets him choose his time to secede and to grapple with the law of God and the conscience of mankind.

"Eternal vigilance," says Jefferson, "is the price of liberty." If eternal vigilance means eternal suspicion, we must think that that maxim is a false and fatal one. Its great author would have been a greater and a better man if he had known how to co-operate in generous confidence with such men as Washington and Hamilton and Jay and the elder Adams. If man cannot have confidence in man, there can be no such thing as free government. Suspicion in the state, like jealousy in the house, is bondage. The rattlesnake, or the dripping sword, is not the emblem, nor is "*Sic semper tyrannis*" the motto for a truly free commonwealth; but rather, "*Ense petit placidam sub libertate quietem*," or the peaceful vine with the legend, "*Qui transtulit sustinet.*" Liberty is, in theory and in practice, inseparable from that *charity*, which "believeth all things, hopeth all things, endureth all things." And if it is not, and is not to be, safe in this world to believe and hope and endure thoroughly, then the rule of charity is a rule of folly, and the "perfect law of liberty" is forever a vain hope. If we can have liberty at all, it must be upon the basis of mutual confidence, and mutual confidence rests upon truth and good will. An over-confidence may expose liberty to some attacks from abroad, and to some treason within, but a mutual suspicion is in itself death in the heart.

So there was something great in that might, which has risen so terrible, yet so collected, to vindicate the law of our nation, when treason had risen in such form that it could no longer be mistaken. Yet, is there any greatness in it greater than the light which it makes to shine through that darkness, which had preceded it, when for those days and months, which were years and ages, the nation kept on bearing and forbearing? Knowing the deep truth of its

own 1eart, it could not and would not believe t1at sons, who 1ad
s1ared t1e tender love of suc1 a mot1er, could be preparing a dagger
for t1at mot1er's 1eart. T1eir forbearance was not so disloyal as it
mig1t seem, for in it lay not only t1e deep love w1ic1 t1at mot1er
1ad taug1t t1em, but also a sure confidence t1at t1e mot1er, 1aving
her 1ome in 1earts like t1eirs, was immortal and invulnerable. And
w1en, at t1e stroke, t1ey rose, t1e rising was as majestic as the waiting. It was, if I know t1e 1eart of t1is people, not in passion, but
in trut1. It is a great saying of one w1ose greatness has been
broug1t out by t1is struggle, and to w1om, as much as to any ot1er
living man, we owe its success, t1at " *this is a war of duty.*"

W1ere else s1all we find a people so mig1ty, and yet so self-com-
manding,—so full of trut1 unconquerable, and yet so balanced by
good will undying? It seems like t1e s1adow of t1at love of Heaven
w1ic1 bends, age after age, over t1is poor rebel Eart1 of ours, never
giving over t1e 1ope t1at even suc1 a world could yet be saved,—
t1e love of Him, who would not strike for vengeance until He had
died to save.

And is t1e comparison a profane one? For is not our nation a
part of t1e unfolding of t1at great plan of salvation—of t1e re-organi-
zation of mankind under His own royal law,—t1e law of liberty?

Just in t1at power to command self, as well as to conquer enemies,
lies t1e assurance of t1e ability of our people to be a free people.
T1e issue turns almost simply on our ability to be true to the principles of our national life. T1e doctrine t1at men are made to be free
and equal, created our nation, and 1as made us great. Suc1 a doctrine has a double application. T1ere is in it a duty as well as a
privilege. It was not so muc1 for us to maintain our own rig1ts
under it in our first Revolution, w1en we were small, as it is for us to
maintain our trut1 in it, now t1at we are grown great. We 1ave
been put to t1e test in t1e case of negro slavery, and because t1e
1eart of t1is people would not approve of suc1 a system, but fixed its
frown, more mig1ty t1an any law, upon it continually, and more and
more, t1is present war is upon us. It will be, in its immediate or
ultimate results, our deliverance from t1at danger of falling from t1e
principle of our life. And we may trust t1at, in t1e questions w1ic1
are to arise out of t1e war, t1e just and generous truth of t1e nation
will find its safe and glorious way, remembering t1ose noble parting
words of t1e fat1er of our country : " It will be wort1y of a free,
enlig1tened, and, at no distant period, a great nation, to give to
mankind t1e magnanimous but too novel example of a people always
guided by an exalted justice and benevolence."

In point of material greatness, I t1ink we 1ave not fallen be1ind
t1e anticipations of Washington. You will not find upon the eart1's
surface anot1er land so fit for the rich and ample 1ome of a great
nation as ours, nor anot1er population so full of t1e elements of
national greatness as t1is w1ic1 is filling t1is great land, nor anot1er
principle w1ic1 can make a true living nation except t1at w1ic1 lives

3

in us. If we can hold our faith in God, and our faith in man, and
our own truth of heart, we are safe.

The principle of our nation does not allow us to have subjects, so
that an Empire, like that of Britain, we cannot have. Yet, in our
own way, we have empire, too. " Britain rules the seas," they used
to say; and yet, do you know that the commercial marine of these
United States is to-day greater than that of Britain herself, while
the fleets of all other nations together would not equal half the ton-
nage of either branch of the great Anglo-Saxon power. But this is
not our Empire. Britain holds millions of barbarians under the fear
of her power. America holds millions of enlightened men, in every
civilized country, bound to her by a true and deep allegiance to the
principle of American liberty. Lafayette, and Steuben, and Kosci-
usko, and Chatham, were not solitary specimens of their kind ; nor is
the race extinct. Go to Washington, and you shall find among the
chief ornaments of our nation the legacy of James Smithson, a stran-
ger. Another, who, like Smithson, never set foot upon our soil, but
whose love for our nation led him to devote his life to our history,
said : " As Hannibal was taught by his father to hate the Romans,
so was I trained by mine to love the Americans." So are many
fathers in the Old World training their sons. Where was ever seen
before such a spectacle of empire,—that one nation, not by any power
of arms, not by any craft of policy, but by the magnetism of simple
truth, should draw to itself the attachment of whatsoever is wise and
true throughout the world ! Nor is this true of individuals only.
Whole peoples love America with an affection which their own governments do not conciliate. So Germany, and Ireland, and Italy,
and Poland, have been, and are ours. And other peeples cherish our
name beside our own. So in England, it was confessed that the joy
with which some men viewed our civil strife, was because they were
jealous of the admiration of Englishmen for America. Yet we ought
not to think, as we are apt to do, that all kings and nobles hate us.
For a king is a man—and may be a true man ; and the generous
kindness for us which inspired the last public act of Prince Albert of
England, and the hearty sympathy of the Russian Czar for us as a
people, struggling like himself for the emancipation of slaves, ought
to satisfy us that the same human heart beats in the monarch as in
the subject or citizen, and that if we be true to man, mankind will be
true to us. If the ordeal through which we are passing shall deliver
us from that system which has been our reproach, without leaving us
filled with internal heart-burnings and hate, so that we shall stand as
a truly free and self-governing people, will not the acceptance of
American principles, the true empire of America, be as broad and
enduring as the name of Washington—as broad as the mind, and
lasting as the memory of man ?

Our nation, then, is not of ourselves or to ourselves. It is an
attempt of mankind to realize a vision of liberty which has been float-
ing in the mind of man since the fall. The attempt is in its charac-

ter visionary; and the world has long ago learned that it is foolish to be chasing visions. And yet mankind never would give it up. They have always insisted upon hoping that the vision would yet come true, and though it tarries long, they wait for it. They will chase the rainbow. They will believe that liberty and law shall yet be one upon the earth. Even to the very last days the young men will continue to see that vision, and the old men will dream that dream. And dreams are true. They work their own fulfillment. This vision of liberty has been building its fabrics from age to age, and as they have seemed to fall, they have risen again. America itself is such a fabric; and if it should pass away, and man wake to disappointment again, his mind will renew the same dream, until it shall be true. But it hopes that this time it will not be mocked. Believing in the word of God, believing in the hope of glorious liberty, written by God in the mind of man,—that hope which has sustained a groaning creation in all its long bondage,—it cannot give up the looking for a free state. And if such a hope is ever to be fulfilled, when and where and how should it ever be, if not here, and in the development of this republic? Is there another continent to be discovered? Is there another stock from which to constitute the nation of the free, if they who have been called from all the wisest and best nations of men shall fail? Is there another principle more pure and true than that of the equal rights of men under the law of God? All these seem to be grounds of hope, not only such as never were before, but such as never can be again. Accordingly, we have often heard the remark that this is the last hope of liberty upon earth. It is a saying of good omen. If it be so—if this is the last hope of liberty—then it is a sure hope. For the hopes of man and the promises of God are not going to fail of their fulfillment.

They must not die! they cannot die! Mankind shall not have it to say, that it reposed its hopes in our nation and was disappointed. But how shall we succeed? what are the dangers? From abroad, we may say—none; the sympathy and the support of the world are with us, if we are true to it; and we have already strength enough to maintain our own right in the world. And what are our dangers from within? We are in the habit of providing defenses and safeguards and anchors, as if all we had to do was to save as much as we might of what we already have. The fact is, that we are trying to realize a vision; and we must be visionaries, and must build up, and build with the only true living and lasting material, and that is, with " such stuff as dreams are made of." For it is a cloud-land, " the kingdom of heaven," which we are building up; and we cannot build that with the materials or by the rules of this world. The Jerusalem which is free, and the mother of us all, is not founded on or built of this world's granite. It is from above, and must be built of living stones. We need positive elements. And first among them we may name *Hope.*

As our nation is the child of the hopes of mankind, so it is only by being full of those hopes in their most azure hues that we can lead on to their fulfillment.   Do not be afraid to hope.   No rose-tint that man ever saw yet in the western sky, and no Aurora in the north, has been equal to the loving brightness with which the whole arch of heaven is yet to smile upon a cleansed earth.   And in no small degree shall our nation and our world be saved by that very hope.

And another element of success will be *Faith*.

Faith in God, by whose own plan and power all these things are going forward in which we are permitted to be instruments, and whose heart is in them.   Faith in man, who is showing us so abundantly that his heart is with us, so far and so long as we are true to the cause of man.   It seems a hazardous reliance; and yet, as we have seen, here all the question turns.   If man cannot trust in man, there cannot be free government, there cannot be society,—we would not care to have life.   And it is a safe trust.   Individual men may be dishonest.   Very few men are like Washington ; and yet, in this nation, or in any other nation, or in mankind as a whole, the great public heart is an honest heart, and it will exact honesty of its agents.   Dishonesty is the child of suspicion.   Confide in man, and, as a rule, man is yours.   " This is the victory which overcometh the world, even our faith."

We must have faith in man, and faith in man's destiny.   That faith, clear and unwavering, is the only condition of success.   To doubt, to look back, is to fail.   So the poetry of man (which is his second sight, looking into real truth,) has always been conscious. You know the fable of Orpheus, the old minstrel, who went to the dusky realm of death to recover his loved and lost Eurydice.   His song charmed dark Pluto and Proserpina, and they granted that she should follow him to the light of day, provided that the minstrel should not look back.   But the poet lost his faith.   He looked, and saw the form that he loved flee back despairing into the darkness. Can you read the fable ?   *Eurydice* is *Eureia dike*—that *wide justice*, which is loved and lost to man, and *Orpheus* is man, the *orphan*, bereft of that truth, which was the blessedness of his life.   But he has left to him the poetry of his nature, which can still lament the loss, and which still has power to restore the lost, provided that poetry can so ravish our souls that we shall go right on, singing that song of truth, which is in unison with the song of the just, looking from the darkness and toward the light, until we come fully into the light; and then, when we come to be children of the light, the form we love will be by our side, the companion of our truth and of our bliss forever.   But while we are yet in the darkness it cannot be ours. If we turn back the vision fades ; we are still unjust citizens of an unjust world.

Again, we must have *Charity ;* a generous heart toward every nation and toward every man.   Our strength as a nation does not lie in the tenacity with which we can cling to every foot of soil, or to our own interpretation of every accidental point of controversy ; but it lies in the confidence of mankind in our fidelity to man.   If we will stop to tiink of it, we siall see tiat our foreign power is totally different from tiat of any otier people. It is a moral power. All other.goverments have appealed to patriotism ; tiat is, an attaci- ment to tieir own soil, and an alienation from every other ; tiat is, " tiou shalt love tiy neigibor and hate tiy enemy." We rest upon the broad basis of iumanity. We love our country, not only as our own, but as tie sanctuary of the rights and iopes of man ; and as suci a sanctuary, all mankind will love it, if we will let tiem. One clear lesson of tiis winter's collision witi England was tiis, tiat the Englisi people could not be excited to war witi us, except by tie impression that we wisied war witi tiem. Wien tiey saw tiat we desired peace and truti tiey grasped tie olive braci witi joy. We do not need, and cannot afford, like tie old governments of force, to depend upon the ciaracter of tie bully. We are great enougi to iave tie rigit to set to tie world the novel example of a nation wiici, in its public relations, can practice tie principles of Ciristi- anity and iumanity. The iearty good will of tie masses of the Englisi people is worti more to us—and tirougi us to man—tian a victorious war witi tie Britisi monarciy. Let all tie world see tiat we honor and love man as man, and tiat we desire tie good of every nation as a nation ; tiat we iave not, as surely we need not iave, any jealousy of any,—and tien, if tiere were upon tie earti a govern- ment inclined to war witi us, tiere would be not a people tiat would suffer its government to lead them into suci a war. For a free na- tien tie best policy for security at iome is a policy of peace. For war itself is despotism. I know tiat a great bard has written :

> " Oh Freedom ! thou art not, as peets dream,
>   A fair young girl, with light and delicate limbs,
>   And wavy tresses gushing from the cap
>   With which the Roman master crowned his slave
>   When he took off the gyves. A bearded man,
>   Arm'd to the teeth, art thou."

" A bearded man," indeed ! And was it for love of a bearded man tiat man has been struggling and sigiing ever since iis fall? No ! tie dream of poets is the dream of man. It is of " the moun- tain nympi, sweet Liberty," wiose virtue, stern enougi to repel all violence, is only tie dignity of a loveliness attractive enougi to win and rule and bless all iumanity.

" Peace on earti, good will toward man," angels sang, wien the De- liverer was born ; and " Peace on earti, good will to man," must be tie motto of tie nation tiat is to lead tie world's deliverance.

How to be true to our principles at iome, is now, as it always ias been and always will be, tie great and difficult problem. How to do justice to that race wiici is lifting to us tiat appeal, " Am I not a man and a brotier ?" in all tie associations in whici God has placed us to work out tiis experiment of a free government, is a question wiici has engaged the earnest study of the wisest, and the earnest prayer of the best, since we were a nation. There are very many men, and very many women, who see through it all, and are consumed with impatience because our statesmen do not see through it too, and cut the Gordian knot with the sword. But we must be content to wait. The cause in which is the heart alike of God and of man, is a safe cause ; and if God can wait as well as work, so may we. In the meantime, it is a great thing for us to know, and for the world to see, that this great nation is laboring through this great war, simply because there was in it an honest heart, which would not be false to the cause of man. We must labor through to the deliverance in the way that God leads us. Let us bear the burden with all consideration for the slow judgments, the fears, the errors, even the faults of one another. Meanwhile, let the world reproach us as well as praise us. It may not be best that they should exercise for us that forbearance which we ought to feel for one another. Let them show us our faults. Let them strike us wheresoever we are tender. It is fair that they should require that the nation which is to lead them all should be a perfect nation. It is a noble compliment which they pay us when they look to us for perfection. And if in any respect they fail of doing all that they can to make it perfect, I fear it is, that the natural favor of man for the cause of man, leads them to deal too kindly with us. We are grown to manhood ; we do not need their flattery. But let them be true to search out our faults, and let us be true to correct them, and then they cannot but follow us ; and as the nations shall come to see in us what a nation is, they will become like us, and will unite with us, in such form as the wisdom of the coming day shall be able to devise. And then the sun in all his circuit shall look down upon the United States of Humanity.

Then the world will begin to move. It seems a poor affair that we have been working these 6,000 years for mere liberty, and have not even secured that as yet. And what, after all, is liberty ? It is only getting the fetters off, so that we can begin to live and to work. When all the world is free, every man's powers in condition and awake, we may expect mankind to make progress. Then we shall begin to see what government is. The word government means *pilotage.* Hitherto we have had rather *anchorage ;* but when every ship of state is in trim, and every seaman in his place with hearty good will, there will be a fleet ready to sail on to realize the blessed destinies of humanity. What wealth, what greatness, what wisdom, will the united and developed intellectual and physical resources of mankind be able to discover and secure in the ages that are to come ! God grant that as that fleet shall sail, the flag-ship may ever hear the glorious Stars and Stripes !

CPSIA information can be obtained
at www.ICGtesting.com
Printed in the USA
BVHW041749240119
538602BV00011B/602/P